Counting
God's Creatures

Published in Nashville, Tennessee, by Oliver-Nelson Books, a division of
Thomas Nelson, Inc., Publishers, and distributed in Canada by
Word Communications, Ltd., Richmond, British Columbia.

Library of Congress Cataloging-in-Publication Data
Mecklenburg, Jan.
    Counting God's creatures / written and illustrated by
  Jan Mecklenburg.
        p. cm.
    ISBN 0-7852-8217-3 (hardcover)
      1. Counting—Juvenile literature. 2. Animals—Juvenile literature.
  [1. Counting. 2. Animals.] I. Title.
  QA113.M45   1994
  513.2'11—dc20   93-36019
  [E]   CIP
                                                    AC

Printed in the United States of America.

1 2 3 4 5 6 — 99 98 97 96 95 94

Counting
God's Creatures

3
7
2
1
6
5

My Very First
Counting and
Rhyme Book

8
4

Written and Illustrated by
Jan Mecklenburg

10
9

THOMAS NELSON PUBLISHERS
Nashville

God made all the little creatures in this land.

God made them with a loving and gentle hand.

God put them here for me to find,
How many creatures of each kind?

1 small snail crawls so very slow.
I wonder where it wants to go.

2 big butterflies flutter by.
First they fly low; then they fly high.

3 great grasshoppers hop along.
I like to hear their chirping song.

4 squirrels sit in a tree.
I see them, but they don't see me.

5 chickadees sing me a song.
I listen, and then I sing along.

6 little rabbits run and play.

Then together they hop away.

7 bees buzz in the clover.
I'm careful to step right over.

8 frogs hop as fast as I run.
How I wish I could catch just one.

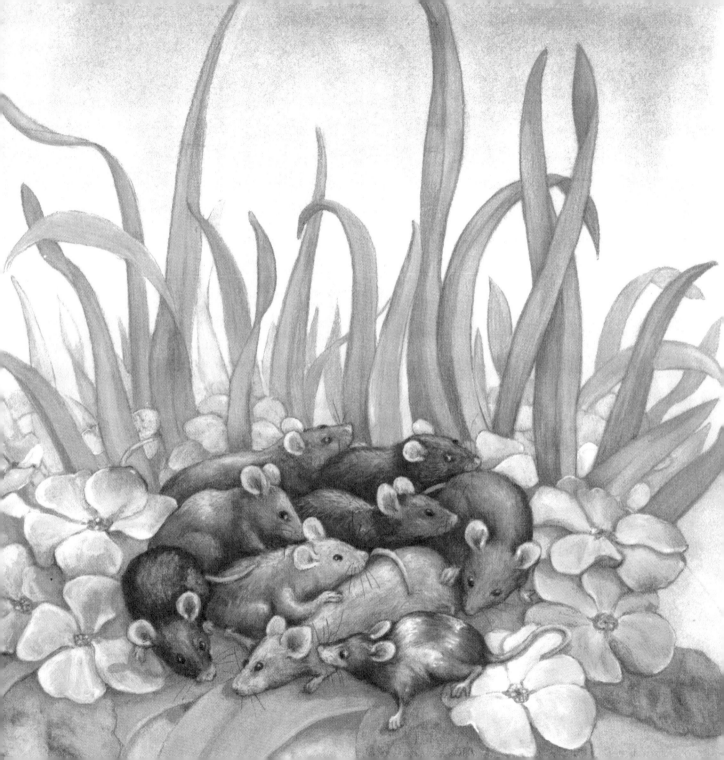

9 mice snuggle up in a ball.
Each one is so fuzzy and small.

10 friendly ducks waddle and quack.
They run away but then come back.

Thank You, God, for giving to me,

The little creatures that I see.

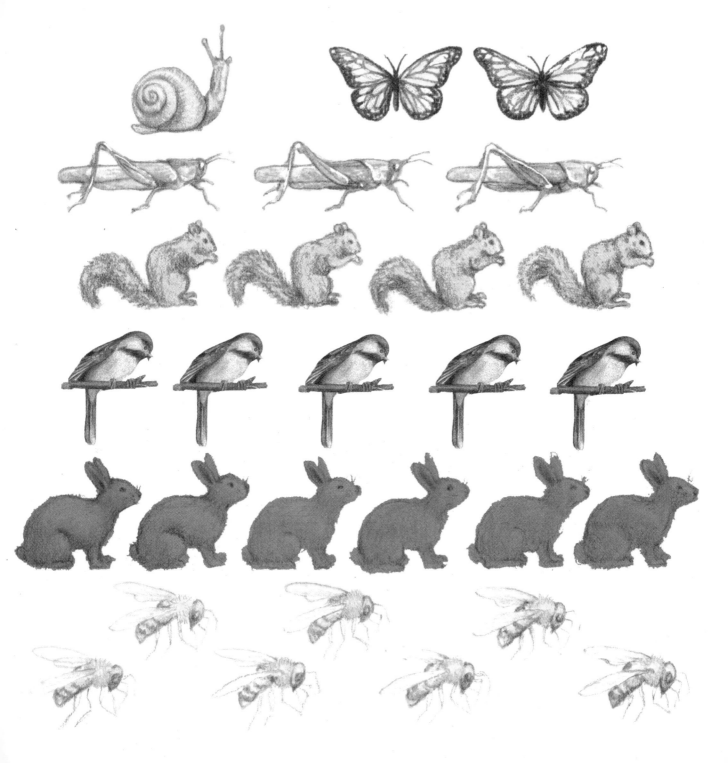